Green Pastures

By

RODDY SHAFFER

Copyright © 2017 Roddy Shaffer Ministries

All rights reserved.

ISBN: 1540797651
ISBN-13: 978-1540797650

DEDICATION

This book is dedicated to all of those out there who are dedicated. To those who are in the fight and desire to fulfill all that God has called them to do. To those who have pressed through hard places, and to those who may be currently facing hard places. One thing is for sure, you are not finished yet.

My desire is that you finish and that you finish strong. That you reach your destiny in Christ, but also enjoy the journey. We all have different courses marked out before us, but the revelation contained in this book will pertain to all that truly have a passion to finish what God has called us to do before the worlds were formed.

CONTENTS

	Acknowledgments	i
1	Propelling Forward	Pg 8
2	Pastures - Plural	Pg 16
3	Green Is Good	Pg 24
4	Out to Eat	Pg 32
5	Here to Get There	Pg 44
6	Going Places	Pg 58
7	Dried up Pastures	Pg 70
8	A Cow at a New Gate	Pg 88
9	New Pasture – New Provision	Pg 102
10	Perfect Pasture	Pg 109

ACKNOWLEDGMENTS

In over twenty years as a believer there have been many truths and revelations that have helped me continue moving forward. There are times that we all need a word from God in due season. A word that will propel us into the next great thing God has for us. It is his word that will be the lamp unto our feet and the light unto our path.

The spoken word became the written word, then the Holy Spirit, by revelation, makes it the Living Word. I believe that the revelation contained in this book will be that word in due season for you! An encouragement to propel you into your high calling in Christ Jesus. You are here, so God can get you there.

GREEN PASTURES

CHAPTER ONE
PROPELLING FORWARD

Our God is a God that is always on the move. If we are going to follow him, then we must move with him. This book is written to all of those that have a passion to finish their race and fulfill what God has called them to do. To those that know the Christian life is more than just church, but a new life 'in Christ'.

God's plan for us all is exceedingly and abundantly far beyond our wildest dreams, hopes and desires. Yet, many settle for less and cease moving forward in their walk with God. They reach a hard place, or maybe a place they don't quite understand and become stagnant. Life for them gets dull and the passion dwindles due to frustration.

Paul had many opportunities to quit and give up. He experienced many difficult and challenging situations. There were many places he found himself that I am sure he had to wonder, 'Why am I in this situation?' He is a great example on how to keep moving forward in the face of difficulty and challenges. We would do well to take heed to Paul's writings. There are some things that he wrote to the church at Ephesus that I believe were written for us today, as he was guided by the Holy Spirit.

Ephesians 1:17-19
17 that the God of our Lord Jesus Christ, the Father of glory, may give to you the spirit of wisdom and revelation in the knowledge of Him, 18 the eyes of your understanding being enlightened; that you may know what is the hope of His calling, what are the riches of the glory of His inheritance in the saints, 19 and what is the exceeding greatness of His power toward us who believe, <u>according to the</u>

<u>working</u> *of His mighty power.*

Then, in the same letter, he wrote in chapter 3:

Ephesians 3:20 Now to Him who is able to do exceedingly abundantly above all that we ask or think, <u>according to the power that works in us</u>.

There are many differing ideas about what the power is that works in us that will propel us into this exceedingly abundant and far above life. However, keeping in context with the letter, I believe that it is the Spirit of wisdom and revelation that will work in us and move us forward in life, propelling us beyond our dreams.

Notice it is the Spirit of wisdom and revelation in the knowledge of him. The Holy Spirit is also called our great teacher. He will work with the word that is in us, then provide wisdom and revelation necessary for us to move forward by applying the word we know. Wisdom is not knowledge, but the ability to apply the knowledge we have. This, in turn, leads us to a life of blessing because it is not the hearer of the word that is blessed, but the doer that is blessed. Paul says that there is a Spirit of wisdom, or application, that will not only teach us doctrine, but how to apply the word in our lives.

The Spirit of Revelation means to reveal or to uncover. God's word is not natural, but it is spiritual. Paul wrote to the Corinthians that the natural man cannot receive spiritual things. Meaning that the truths of God's word cannot merely be understood with our intellect alone. They must be enlightened and illuminated to our Spirit. The Holy Spirit will take the spoken word that was written, then by revelation reveal it to our spirit, thus we have a Living Word.

We need the helper as we search God's word for our daily lives. Helping us to see radical truths that will become for us daily spiritual food. Without him we will not see things intended for us to see. If Paul prayed this for the church of Ephesus, then it is a prayer we should pray for ourselves. There are hidden truths and revelations in the word likened to treasures to be searched for. These treasures are not hidden from us, but they are hidden for us. Daily uncovering treasures of truth that will transform our lives beyond our imagination. Discovering new valuable nuggets daily as we search God's eternal word.

Jesus said, 'Seek and you will find' and

'the hungry will be filled'. As we search God's word and pray that the Spirit of wisdom and revelation come alongside to help us, he will be faithful and keep us moving forward. There is excitement and passion in living the life God has called us to live. The path you and I are on is a path filled with great treasure. God's treasure map leading us forward to all the good stuff.

I am sure we have all heard the phrase, "One word from God can change your life forever." Isn't that amazing? Only one word from God can completely change the course and destiny of a person's life. A missionary can hear one word, 'Go!', and their life is forever changed. Peter had one word, 'Come!', and he moved out on that word and did the impossible, walking on water. The power of God's word that is alive and active in us propels us to do things beyond what we could naturally do. In this life, you are going to need that power working in your life to move forward and continue. In our strength, we become weary and faint. We were never intended to live life in our own strength. We are moved forward daily, empowered daily, and renewed daily by a supernatural God, revealing his supernatural word in us and working to carry us to his supernatural plan and purpose.

I have found myself many times in difficult places. I have had the temptations to quit and to give up many times before. However, there has been one nugget of truth that I have kept in my pocket along the way that has helped me to continue and move forward. It was not one word from God, but it was simply one letter revealed by the Holy Spirit that I will be forever grateful! Imagine, a word so alive that one letter can contain enough power to propel you and move you forward in God's great plan. One letter can bring you encouragement even in the most discouraging time. One letter can bring clarity in hard to understand circumstances and situations. One letter from God's word is what the rest of this book is based upon. A whole book written on only one letter from God's powerful word. It changed my life when the Holy Spirit uncovered it for me and I believe it will do the same for you.

I am so thankful to be able to share this truth that the Lord showed me years ago. My prayer is that it will help to propel you into a life beyond your wildest hopes and dreams.

CHAPTER TWO
PASTURES - PLURAL

Psalms 23:1 The Lord is my shepherd; I shall not want. 2 He makes me to lie down in green pastures; He leads me beside the still waters.

Finding myself in an extremely hard situation and on the verge of quitting the Lord revealed to me a truth from Psalms 23 that drives me and continues to motivate me. To this day, the illumination of one letter keeps me pressing forward toward God's high calling. We all have our own course to run. That course for all of us includes a beginning, a middle and an ending. Our goal is to run through the finish line victorious, having done all that God created us to do.

God's word is so alive that one letter has continuously helped me, time and time again.

Many that are reading this are most likely believers. Hopefully believers that intend to walk out God's purpose and his plan completely. Many have that desire, but sadly fall short of walking out that plan. In being open and transparent, there have been many times in my life that I could have walked away from that plan instead of walking out that plan. Experiencing many hard times just making sense of everything going on in life. Trying to figure out why God has me right here right now?

In my case, I found myself in a job that did not make sense to me at all. I remember asking, "Is this really what God has for me?" I knew God, and he had been so good to me in my short walk with him. He had far exceeded any thought I had of him. I went from a lost drunk person that was propelled into my dream of coaching high school basketball. For three years, I coached there and God did amazing things in those three years. Revival broke out at that high school and ninety percent of the school voluntarily began attending a Bible study during their lunch hour. For me, it could not have been any better.

Then, suddenly, it all changed! The coaching job came to an end and now I found myself working at a pest control company killing bugs. Doing anything I could to help provide for my new bride. Was I happy? Not at all. I'd have to say that I was really confused at this point in my life. I thought many times that God might be confused as well. I read the word every day, studied the word and believed I was following God in all the decisions that I had made thus far. Surely there had to be an answer. Surely there had to be a reason I went from living my dream to a job that I just couldn't figure out?

While I was riding shotgun in the truck with the other bug killing technicians I always had my pocket Bible with me. I would read as we drove all day on a mission to rid the world of roaches. It was my most favorite pocket bible that I ever owned. It was not just the new testament, but the new and old testament. While riding on an old country rode in North Louisiana I was reading Psalms 23 in that Bible, and my life changed forever.

Psalms 23:1 The Lord is my shepherd; I shall not want. 2 He makes me to lie down in green pastures...

Then I heard on the inside, *'You are where you are, so I can get you to where you are going.'* Then everything around me went silent. The other person talking and the radio playing, all sounds were muted while the Holy Spirit took me to class. Then he focused on that one letter – "s".

He said, 'Did you notice that there are many pastures and not just one?' Then he began to reveal to me that 'green' referred to places where you can grow the most. 'I am growing you here, so that you will be ready when you get there.' This was all starting to become illuminated to me while we were riding on those back roads and I couldn't wait to get home to dig into this even deeper.

My thought, as a new believer, was that you get born again and now become the sheep of his pasture. I had pictured in my mind a luscious green pasture where all of God's children graze and feed. Now this one letter, 's', had opened to me a revelation that the pastures God leads you to he leads you there to grow you there. Once you have grown there and gotten everything you can from that pasture, he opens the gate to a new pasture. God leads us to pasture's' of growth, and does not just drop us off to fend for ourselves to make our own way. Each pasture is strategic placement. 'You are where you are, so I can get you to where you are going.'

That statement may not have meant much to others at that time, but it was a word in due season for me. My confusion was real at the time. Why did the coaching job, that I loved, come to an end? Why did God's plan include closing that chapter? Then he said, 'You got everything from that pasture that you could get, now I have other places of growth that I am taking you.'

Looking back at those three years in that high school it all became clear. I arrived there one year after getting born again. God opened that door because of my passion to coach. While there he began to develop, and grow in me an all new passion, to minister God's word. The daily Bible studies required me to study the word daily and prepare to give it out every day at lunch to the students. I didn't know it at the time, but I was growing and developing at a phenomenal rate just being in the green pasture God had led me to.

After arriving back home from a long day of bug killing and Holy Spirit one on one revelation class it was time to set aside the time and get everything out of this 'green pastures' revelation that I could. What I would receive from this one letter would prove to change how I viewed every aspect of my life. It would change my attitude while in every new pasture that God led me to. It would bring purpose to every step, by knowing that it is all about the process and journey, not just the destination.

God has many stages of your development. Though you may not understand them all at the time, if he led you here, He is growing you here to get you there!

CHAPTER THREE
GREEN IS GOOD

Psalms 23:1 The Lord is my shepherd; I shall not want. 2 He makes me to lie down in <u>green</u> pastures…

As I began to seek out more wisdom and revelation, and had my notebooks spread across the bed, the one word that stood out was 'green'. God does not just lead us to pastures, but he leads us to green pastures. While meditating on this, I asked the Holy Spirit, 'What is a green pasture?' He responded, 'It is a place that you can grow the most.'

In Jeremiah 29:11 God says that he knows the plans he has for you, plans to prosper you and not to harm you. This word prosper is often misunderstood by much of the church world. Many see prosperity only in reference to finances and provision. However, when you do a word study it means to move forward and to advance. Provision becomes a result of the advancing and moving forward. It comes because of prospering and advancing. Prospering is not receiving things, but moving forward and advancing, then by forward movement you enjoy provision along the way.

In God's plan to advance you he first places you strategically and begins to grow you. When we are in God's plan and following his leading there is always going to be growth and development. God does not lead you any place that he does not feed you. We may not understand what God is doing at the time, or why he has you in the pasture that he has, but he has a plan. That plan includes growth and development. It is a place you will grow the most. It is a place that you are developing for that season of your life.

Often, we can determine if we are following God's leading by how green the pasture is that we find ourselves. If there is nothing but dried up pasture land around you and there is no growth potential and all seems dead, God did not lead you to that place. We cannot, however, determine if we are in the right place simply by feelings of not wanting to be there. Sometimes children do not want to eat things that they need to eat. What they want is not always what they need. If it were left to them they would prefer a pasture full of candy. However, candy does not provide nourishment needed for development and growth.

Deuteronomy 8: 7 For the Lord your God is bringing you into a <u>good land</u>, a land of brooks of water, of fountains and springs, that flow out of valleys and hills; 8 a land of wheat and barley, of vines and fig trees and pomegranates, a land of olive oil and honey; 9 a land in which you will eat bread without scarcity, in which you will lack nothing.

God brings you into a good land where there are provisions and where there is no lack. God's plan is good and where he leads us is for our good. Green pastures are good pastures. God knows what is good for us even when we may not know what is good for us. Allowing him to bring us to the good land and following his leading will always prove to be good. It may not always be easy but it will always be good.

I have said it often, 'If living by faith

were easy then everyone would do it.' Too often we make the mistake and think that we are in the wrong place if it is a difficult place. But those difficult places can also be places of our greatest growth and development, making them very good places. We can see this throughout God's word. God led Paul into places that were not easy, but they were places that he would grow and in turn it would grow the entire body of Christ.

Faith steps are good. God's leadings are always good. He is always bringing us to good lands and places he desires for us to eat without scarcity. If God brought you there then there is something eternal that God is doing in you there.

While I was in the high school coaching pasture that God brought me to he did so many good things in that land. Prior to getting in that pasture of development I was a mere baby in Christ. I had no experience in leadership, no real experience in working alongside of a staff and no experience in public speaking. When that pasture dried up I had grown in leadership, developed at working alongside others and speaking before crowds was developed daily.

God was growing me and the pasture was green. I was in a land that I could grow the most and he would develop me there so he could get me where I was going. Sure, I would have been content staying in that pasture forever, but then I would have missed out on all the great things he would later bring me to. In his divine wisdom, he knew that one day I would Pastor a church, lead people and often preach on a daily basis. This was a necessary pasture for me to prepare me for where I was going. It was not always easy and there were many challenges along the way, but today I thank God for that pasture of development. There are still things I use today that God grew in me then.

When you know that where God has you is for his good purpose and only for your good it helps you to appreciate the process. Do not become discouraged when difficulties arise. Always be mindful that God is doing a good work in you and the work that he is doing in you is better than the things he could do for you. God is not in control of how well you fare in the green pastures, often it is our attitude that will determine how rapidly we grow.

Green is good! God is good! He only has good that he is doing for you and in you at every pasture. Don't allow the difficult or challenging times to keep you from enjoying the journey God is taking you on. Take it all in with a thankful attitude knowing that God is up to a lot of good. Be grateful and know that though you are not where you want to be, you are not where you once were. It is a good thing to follow God's good plan.

CHAPTER FOUR
OUT TO EAT

Psalms 23:1 The Lord is my shepherd; I shall not want. 2 He makes me to lie down in green pastures...

How many first dates are going out to eat? I know that my wife and I met on a blind date, set up by a girl in the high school I was coaching at, and that first date was going out to eat. I think it is cool that as soon as the Lord becomes your shepherd and your leader he takes you out to eat. He not only takes you out to eat, he leads you to the very best. This first pasture that he leads us to is a strategic and very important first date. I like to call it the baby pasture or baby stage that we all must go through.

Danielle and I have two children, Julia and Jake. Though they are both very different there is one thing that was the same about both as babies, all they did was eat. When they were through eating, then they would eat some more. They enjoyed eating and it was necessary for them to grow. They still eat every day and they are still growing every day. However, in the baby and the toddler years they just took it all in. They would try to eat just about anything. They would chew on magazines, hammers, keys and just about anything they could get in their mouth. I'm sure some of that had to do with teething, but everything was going in the mouth that was for sure.

I recall my baby stage in Christ and how I just wanted to take it all in. I would hear a sermon and just eat it up. I would open the Bible and it was all brand new to me and it was good. I wanted to feed more on faith, righteousness, healing, prosperity, peace, joy and anything else that was in God's good word. If you put it in front of me I was just ready to eat it.

Jeremiah 15:16 Your words were found, and I ate them, And Your word was to me the joy and rejoicing of my heart

When the Lord takes us out to eat he feeds us his good word and it brings a joy and rejoicing to the heart. We can all remember how we could not wait to get more. That was Jake's first word, 'More, more, more!' Not Momma or Daddy, but more! He wanted more! More made him happy!

This is something that we cannot lose in our walk with the Lord. A hunger for more! He will never stop taking us out to eat. If you look later in Psalms 23 he is also setting a table before us just after we made it through the valley of the shadow of death. He takes us out to eat in preparation for the valley, then he fills us up again after we go through the valleys. Why? His word is the strength of our life. Without it we will not develop and we will not grow.

Sadly, many people start off taking in all of God's good word by feeding continuously, then they stop feeding and stop eating. Growth stops and development stops for them because in every green pasture we must never stop feeding. The moment that we neglect to feed on God's amazing word is the moment we lose our strength to fulfill God's purpose and his plan. His word is supernatural strength and nourishment for our spirit man. He first takes us out to eat because he knows how badly we need it for everything he has called us to do.

When I was growing up we had a pasture beside our house, and in that pasture we had a cow. We did not have a hundred head of cattle, we only had that one cow. We got the cow when it was only a baby calf and had special bottles we used to feed it. I can remember to this day how badly that food smelled that we had to mix in that huge baby bottle container with that long nipple on the end. We were not extremely faithful in going out there to feed that calf and our Dad worked away from home a lot. There would be times that poor calf just looked shriveled up and malnourished. Daddy would come home and begin ranting and raving, 'Have you been feeding that cow?' It was obvious we had not been doing our chores.

When a calf is in a pasture it doesn't always mean that they are eating everything that they need to eat. That calf needed the things that were in that special mixture or it would not fully develop. With us it is much the same, there are some things that we need for us to grow, especially in our baby stage of development. Failing to feed on God's word continually in our baby pasture makes us malnourished and weak, and often it is the main cause many never advance and develop into other pastures.

That calf did eventually, somehow, grow into a cow. Yet, it always seemed to have issues when it came to feeding, maybe it was from its rough childhood. We had that cow fenced into a pasture that was roughly two acres. The fence was a wooden fence with four rows of thick round poles that ran horizontal.

That crazy cow had everything it needed in that two-acre pasture. A big water trough and all the green grass one cow could ever need. But it never failed, usually weekly we would get a call from our neighbor, Mr. Sullivan, 'Your cow is hung up in the fence, his head is stuck and he can't get free.' What was he trying to do? He was trying to feed on the grass that was outside the pasture, by stretching his neck through the wooden fence and somehow, he would get stuck.

All the green grass a cow could eat, with no other cows to share it with, and he still wanted to see if the grass was better on the other side. This got him in a bind repeatedly. Everything was there he needed in the pasture we put him, but he thought there may be better stuff out there.

Where God places you to feed on his word there is enough there to keep you eating for a long time. Don't fall for the temptation that there may be something better out there somewhere. Often it is only a trap to get you stuck in the fence. Why? When God takes you out to eat there is plenty in that pasture that will grow you and strengthen you. When the time comes for grazing elsewhere he will open the gate and take you to the new pasture that is just for you. Don't become distracted by the curiosity of what is going on in other pastures. Those other pastures are not where God has taken you out to eat. Can you imagine someone taking you out to eat, then you begin going to eat from someone else's table? Just wandering off and trying to eat what was ordered for someone else.

That may seem like an extreme example, but I have seen many start in their place God has them, then veer off into another place not designated for them. They may start feeding on faith filled teaching, then some new age teaching moves in next door. They decide they are going to test it out and ultimately, they get hung up in the fence and in a personal struggle, then you have to go and help them get unstuck.

It's funny that sometimes there are new believers recently been born again, and in six months they are talking about how God has been teaching them about the mark of the beast and end times revelations. They have it figured out when Jesus is coming back and they are eager to tell everyone that will listen. No! That is not on a baby's menu, they are eating off the wrong menu. They have yet to learn who they are in Christ, but they have become an expert in eschatology, and are not even a one year old believer.

When God takes you out to eat, keep your head down while feeding and just take in everything in your pasture you can. Avoid distractions and what may be going on in another person's pasture. God will always lead you to feed on the green healthy word he has just for you. You will avoid getting hung up in the fence and you will enjoy the place that God taken you to. He only dines at the finest of places. You can go 'out to eat' with him every day. There are no left overs and it is fresh every day.

My wife did not understand me when we first got married. I informed her early on in our marriage that I did not eat leftovers. To this day there are only certain things that I will re-heat and eat again, like spaghetti, which is good after it marinates for a while. I would rather have a fresh peanut butter and jelly than an old casserole that has been in the fridge for a few days.

I think that is one reason I really love God's way of feeding us. It is always fresh and never stale. Even when he fed the children of Israel in the wilderness, the food was good for one day, then it went bad. Nobody wants leftover quail and manna. He gives us daily our daily bread. Not that he only gives just enough, but that what he gives is always fresh. I have never grown tired of what God feeds me daily. It is always hot and fresh! When he takes you out to eat he is not re-heating some leftovers. It is always good and he always knows what needs to be on your daily menu. He wants you full and satisfied at all times because he knows what you have coming ahead. You will need to be well fed and fueled up for the journey that lies before you.

Our shepherd leads us and feeds us only the best! Keep your head down and focus on what he sets before you. Eat what is on his menu for that day, because he wants to take you out to eat every day. This is something that never stops, he will be taking you out to eat daily at every stage, the rest of your life and you are sure to enjoy it!

CHAPTER FIVE
HERE TO GET THERE

'You are where you are, so I can get you to where you are going.'

Now that you are continually feeding your spirit man to remain strong for the journey, there are other reasons that you are where you are. You cannot be there just to eat, doing so you may just get fat and lazy. In every pasture, God wants us to eat right and exercise. Just like our natural man needs to eat right and exercise, so does our spirit man.

You are where you are right now to grow and to develop. What you do here will determine when you move on to the next great thing God has for you. Our promotion to the next green pasture is completely based on how well we are developing in the pasture right now. This is where I began to realize that if I was going to move on from the place I was in then I would have to make some changes in my attitude.

You see, promotion to the next pasture is not something that takes place yearly or at a certain physical age. It is all based on development and growth. Just because a person has a call of God on their life to do great things does not mean that they will ever do anything. God rewards one thing, and it is faithfulness. Those faithful over a few things get promoted to much. So, what does that mean for those that are not faithful with the few things? They are not promoted until they can prove faithful.

Once I saw this truth clearly and realized that I could remain in the place I was in based entirely on how I treated the here and now, I began to want to grow and develop rapidly. My new outlook was if I was going to be there, then be all there. Meaning if I was there for growth and development then let's get growing! Why be only half here and not all here?

We must realize that God is not going to promote us onto new and exciting things simply because of our talent and anointing. When we do, we will become serious with our development while being in the place God has us.

Soon after my six months of bug killing days were over I moved on to another green pasture that God led me to. I had a friend of mine that was the chaplain of a boys' home in our local area. He had told me of all the opportunities to minister to these boys that were taken from their families by the state. These boys needed the word of God in a major way. I visited the boys' home and went into the office to speak to the owner of the facility. He was very eager to see me walk in and had heard about all the great things that had taken place at the high school where I had coached. He said that they would love to have me there working with the boys at the ranch.

Times were hard at the house and much tension had developed. I went from the coaching job, then to killing bugs, then was out of work for over a month. On the same day, I was offered the job at the boys' ranch I also had another interview lined up for a sales position. Often, I had been told that I was a natural salesman and needed to be in sales. Usually someone would hear me preach and decide that the communication gift would be a good fit for sales. After a service at church one day I was talking to a man that owned a local company and he invited me to come for an interview. Since I was out of work and spending all my time praying and reading the word I figured that I needed to take all the interviews I could.

After leaving the first interview at the boys home I was stirred in my spirit about helping them any way I could. However, the owner of the ranch said the only thing available at the time was a minimum wage position as a case worker in the dorm with the boys. Well, five dollars per hour was not exciting at the time and I was off to interview number two. When I sat down at this interview the owner dropped a W-2 in front of me of the sales person that had just left the company. It was well over six figures and definitely better than minimum wage. He looked at me and said, 'I believe you could do better than that on accident.' I left there and returned home excited about the interview. When Danielle got home she said, 'How did the interviews go?' I told her about them both and she said, 'Well, that's easy, you'd be miserable in that sales job for sure. You know what to do.' So, the next green pasture for me would be a minimum wage position working with abandoned and abused boys.

After a month of being there and being around a lot of the other minimum wage workers with bad attitudes, talking down to the boys and mistreating them, I was beginning to question this pasture. I was going to work at six o'clock and coming home at two o'clock in the afternoon, barely making enough money to pay even a few bills. I was discouraged and driving to the ranch one morning said, 'Why am I even here?' Then a still small voice on the inside said, 'So you can get there.' It was all that I needed to hear and from that day forward I would not have a bad attitude in the place that God had me. I decided I would be there, and I would be all there.

As a minimum wage case worker, I began to take every opportunity to do what I knew God had me there to do, which was minister faith and hope to boys who had none. I asked if we could start a Bible study on a night that was not normally set aside for their chapel services. They of course said yes, and we started with five boys coming to the bible study. After two months, all 70 boys at the ranch were coming and filling the chapel. An all-boys choir was started that would eventually go out and sing in local churches. We redesigned the old chapel they had into a cool youth facility for the boys. That Christmas we organized for all the boys to get brand new nice shoes sponsored by local businesses in the area. We even had local bands come in and play during our services.

After months of being all there and being all in while I was there a very neat thing occurred. My friend that was the chaplain there was starting a church and was going to move into full-time at the church. When he left the ranch, he requested that I be offered the job as full-time chaplain. I was called in and offered the position and offered a raise for more than triple what I was making before. Not only that, but I was also asked to be a part of the training for all new staff being hired. It would be a requirement that all new hires go through an hour-long class with me for five days and basically be trained in the word of God before entering a dorm. We had many new hires that received salvation and were born again in our training sessions.

The time eventually came that God said, 'You've gotten all that I intended for you in that pasture, it's time to move on.' And it was just getting fun! But, I knew now that if he was moving me it was only to another good green pasture that would be the best for me.

What I learned there in that pasture at the boys' home was invaluable. There were so many things that God worked in me, and so many ways that he grew me, that if I had not gone through that pasture I would not be here doing what I do today. How I treated that place and time in my life fully determined if I would qualify for the next thing that God had in store.

You may be serving in the local church and in a developmental stage of growth. How you treat that place God has you will determine if you move on to the next place awaiting you. If you are there, then be all there. Be there with a great attitude and superior work ethic. Do everything that you can to be impressive and to display excellence to everyone watching. You will get the most out of the pasture God has you in, when you make the most of the pasture God has you in.

You may be waiting tables, working in a sales position, or nursing at a local hospital. It is up to you how you treat that place that God has led you to. With a halfhearted treatment of that pasture then you can expect an extended stay in that place. God does not just go to church with us, he goes everywhere with us. Notice that none of the examples I have used thus far have been examples that were in the church, but were outside the church.

God develops us and grows in our secular work as well. Developing skills and talents that will be needed for the future pastures of life. If we limit God to our church activity, we will miss most of his work in our life. God has grown and developed me just as much in the secular work force as he has while I served in the local church. I developed more skills away from church than I ever did at church. My time coaching, my time administrating at the boy's home, my time working as director of a public-school outreach, my time owning my own business with nine employees; these played a larger role in developing and preparing me for where I am today than hearing sermons in church. It was the growth and development there that became useful in the church.

When referencing new pastures and promotion to new things, I believe it's important to note that this does not always mean moving jobs or careers. In the church, it does not mean that everyone is working to be promoted to a staff position or pastor. It could be that you proved extremely faithful and developed in an ushering position by making the most out of time served there. Then God promotes you to a head usher pasture for more leadership. You then develop in that place and God uses you to develop a training program for ushers in the church. Then another gate opens and an opportunity to travel and develop the usher departments for other churches. Then after proving faithful in all the above then you begin to publish usher's curriculum and a book on how volunteering to usher at church changed your whole life.

This same type of scenario could even be used in the secular work place. You could be an RN at a hospital that gets noticed by the administration at the hospital. Your work ethic is admired from afar then you are asked to lead training classes and leadership courses. You are still nursing, but you are now doing it at another level. It is the same job as before but now God is growing different skills in you for leadership. You then have a stirring in your heart to publish a book on how learning to work with people will result in learning to lead people. Then you become a nationwide nurse with a bestselling book and influence millions of people.

These are both simple examples and neither include someone working their way to become pastor so that they could feel like a successful believer. Both examples never get any pulpit time and never preach a sermon at a church. They are just people that are doing all they can here and God is able to move them there.

What happens next depends on what happens now.

CHAPTER SIX
GOING PLACES

2 Corinthians 3:18 (KJV)
18 But we all, with open face <u>beholding</u> as in a glass the <u>glory</u> of the Lord, are <u>changed</u> into the same image <u>from glory to glory,</u> even as by the Spirit of the Lord.

God's desire for all his children is growth and change. Change can often be hard on people. We are creatures of comfort and many times do not respond well when our routine is changed. We want increase and we desire greater things in life, but if nothing changes, then nothing changes.

The scripture above shows that glory to glory is promised to us as followers of Jesus. Not only is it promised, I believe that God expects it in our life. It is the process of one good place to another good place, one glorious place to another glorious place. Walking with the good shepherd, he takes us from one good thing to another good thing. This is one of the greatest promises for a believer, but it is not automatic and does not just happen because it is God's plan.

3:18 But we all, with open face <u>beholding</u> as in a glass the glory of the Lord, are <u>changed</u>

The word beholding means to look at intently and deeply. The example that is used is a glass, or a mirror. To look intently into God's mirror, beholding him and changing progressively into his image. This is not a passing glance, nor is it a brief look at the mirror of God's word, but an intense deep look into God's perfecting word.

My wife, Danielle, has a mirror she uses when she is changing and getting ready to go out. It is a double-sided mirror that has a side that acts as a normal mirror, then the other side a magnifying mirror. The magnifying mirror also has a light all around it to illuminate everything that is being magnified. I looked into that mirror one time and I could see down into the pores on my face. A closer and a deeper look, this is what it means to behold.

She does not use this mirror all the time, but at times that we are going places she uses it before changing. Likewise, we are going places with God, from glory to glory, but change is required. Before change occurs, a deep intense beholding is required. If we neglect the beholding, then we will also neglect the change required. This is something that we must do, and not something that God is going to do for us. God's word shows us the new creation and who we were designed to be. When you look into a mirror you see what the mirror is saying back to you. God's mirror is designed to, not only show you Jesus, but also to show you the new you that you were created to be. God sees you how he said you are, now he wants us to behold intently this new creation. The more we look at ourselves how God says that we are, the more our lives transform and change. The more we change, the more places he can take us. Before God can take us, he must make us.

This beholding for us is a focus that we must maintain while in the pasture God has placed us. A sheep with our head down, feeding and growing taking it all in. Making every necessary change that is required to take us to the next glory. Intense about where God has us, knowing that he is taking us places. We are where we are, so that he can get us to the place we are going. Staying intently focused and keeping our head down fixed on the task at hand we will grow supernaturally.

Matthew 4:19 Then He said to them, "Follow Me, and I will make you fishers of men." 20 They immediately left their nets and followed Him.

As our shepherd, Jesus leads and feeds. As his sheep, we follow and swallow. God's word shows us a long list of natural people God called to follow him, it is amazing to see what he made them and the places that he took them. These fishermen in the scripture above were going about their day and doing their thing. The great I AM showed up in their life and everything radically changed when they dropped everything to follow him. He took normal fishermen and made them into world changers. He took these men that were going nowhere and for the rest of their lives they were men that were going places.

As God takes you places, his intent is to make you and form you into his will for your life. Change was a requirement for these lifelong fishermen. They had to decide that it would be better to leave their old life behind completely and follow the one that held the blueprint for their life, they did this immediately. These were not casual fishermen, they were fishermen as an occupation. They had spent a lifetime of making themselves the best fishermen they could be. Then, along comes Jesus, with a proposition to leave all they had made themselves, and let him remake them. How? He would take them on a journey. When God takes you to walk with him, he is doing it with a purpose of remaking you.

Immediately they left their nets and followed him. They left the only way of life that they had ever known and invited the changes that Jesus offered. A decision that they would never regret. A change that was not easy, but was necessary in God's great plan. Changes are necessary when we are going from glory to glory with the great shepherd. Dropping the old and laying it down is an act of trust and an act of faith.

The one thing that prevents us from

going glory to glory with God is fear of change. We like to call it comfort zones, but it is fear of change. And fear is not comfortable, it is only an excuse that keeps us from change. When Jesus walked on the water to the disciples the Bible says that they were in the boat and fearful when they saw him. Peter then stepped out on one word, 'Come!', many say that the others stayed in their comfort zone, but the Bible says that they were filled with fear. Fear paralyzes us from moving out in faith and going places that we have never gone before. Stepping out in faith 'makes' us water walkers and capable of doing things we have never done before.

As we grow with God it will be the result as we go with God. Yes, change will be required for us all, but it is good change. Embracing change and becoming a person that welcomes it will take you places with God. Faith is acting on the word with no evidence in the visible realm; we walk by faith and not by sight. Faith comes by hearing, but is not complete faith until it goes and is acted upon. 'Faith that cometh and does not goeth is deadeth.'

This journey for us all is a faith journey. Along the way, God is taking us and making us. It is never to be for us a boring life, but a life filled with excitement and a life of growth. You may have never been there before, but if God is taking you there then it is a great place. You will see things that you have never seen and you will do things that you have never done. All the disciples that stayed in the boat could only preach about what they watched Peter do, yet none of them were water walkers themselves. As you walk with God you will be able to share your own stories of how God took you and made you something you never dreamed you could become. You will become an encouragement to those that are fearful of change. People will see that following God does not cost, but it pays. They will see that God is taking you places and he can take them places as well. Our life going from glory to glory is attractive to those that have become fearful of change.

If you know that you have been following God to get you where you are right now and feel like nothing is happening there, make sure that you are all there. Your role in every place God sends you is to give yourself wholly and completely while you are there. You are surrounded with God's favor, but you must win the favor of man. This means you should do everything that you do with all your heart, working as unto the Lord and not unto man. Doing this will cause you to win the favor of man, then God can speak to men's hearts to help get you to the place you belong. Live your life in such a way that you are impressive to everyone around you. Evaluate yourself and ask yourself hard questions; Do I impress myself with my efforts? If I were the boss would I promote my efforts? Should I expect to hear, 'Well done, good and faithful servant'? Are there potentials in me that have yet to be revealed in this current pasture?

Joseph not only found favor with God, but he won the favor of man due to how he did all things well. God's plan all along was that he be promoted to second in charge of all the land. Yet, if he had lost his passion to do everything that it took for him to reach his high calling, he would have never come out of the pit and made it to the palace. Our destiny was written before the foundations of the world, but they are not guaranteed.

Before getting frustrated and laying down on the plan God has for you, ask yourself serious questions. Could it be that you are giving half efforts and unimpressive performances? Before bailing out and leaving the course God has set before you, you owe it to yourself, and to God, to give it your best efforts. Get locked in and become intense in the task before you. Get everything that you can out of this current pasture. It is often just a simple heart adjustment that leads to promotion and advancement.

CHAPTER SEVEN
DRIED UP PASTURES

As a man that enjoys eating, it is a very frustrating thing when there is nothing in the house to eat. That can often become the case, because a hungry man can go through groceries very rapidly. There may be some things in the pantry but not really anything you like, or that you are hungry for at the time. I have even made many trips to the grocery store long after everyone else has gone to sleep in our house because what I was looking for was not in the house.

I have found that God will lead us into new pastures once we have taken in all we can take in where we are. We often get frustrated in a place because there is nothing there for us any longer. We were so busy with our head down eating everything and growing in the place God had us that we look up and see that there's not a lot more to get out of that pasture.

My first year of coaching school basketball everything was abundant all around me and the growth was new every day. The second year that I was there I was in the prime of my development in many ways. However, the third year, it all began well and fine, then during the middle and end of that year I became frustrated. I could not tell you specifically why I was frustrated, but I just knew something was different. The students were still the same, they were growing and developing in sports and in the daily bible studies at lunch time, but it was not them, it was me. There was something frustrating in me that was the issue. I still had a daily platform to minister to the entire school and that was a great thing. Yet, there was a frustration building in me that I was not quite sure what it was. When it came to the end of the year, I remember the Lord saying to me, 'You have gotten all that I wanted you to get out of this pasture. It's time to move on.'

The growing and development there was over. Yes, I was still in a pasture, but it was no longer a green pasture for me. I had taken in all that I could take in and developed as much as I could develop in that coaching position. Now, I could sense a time of transition and began to understand the frustration that I felt on the inside. It was not the people around me, but it was God doing something in me. Teaching me how to transition from one pasture to another. Transition time can be a difficult time, but staying in a place that you are not growing any longer can be even more difficult.

I know many people that stayed too long in one place. They became frustrated there, not because that place was bad, but because they could no longer grow there. Sadly, many people live in these dried up pastures the rest of their life and it becomes for them a life of frustration. We all know people that wake up dreading the day because they feel like their job is taking from them, instead of them taking from and growing from their job. If the only thing that your job is giving you is a check and it has no longer become a growing and developmental pasture, then it could be that you have gotten everything from that pasture.

The good news is that God has more for you! The fact that he leads us to 'pastures' means that we always have more to look forward to in our life. When one dries up for us it does not mean that it is the end, it only means that there must be something great just ahead.

While at the youth ranch, when I decided to put my head down and focus on the growth God placed me there for, what began as a place I did not want to be turned into a place I did not want to leave. The fruit was enormous, not only for the ranch, the boys and the staff, but also in my personal growth and development. I had received a raise based on performance there, and was still able to accomplish other outside ministry opportunities the Lord had opened to me. Then after about two years in that position, when everything seemed to be going great, a frustration began to arise from within. I had no need to be frustrated on the outside, things looked great. I was ministering to the boys, the staff, ministering in public schools, ministering at our home church and could even set my own schedule. Why was I becoming frustrated with this place that I was in that seemed to be everything that I desired? Then, I heard those words, 'You have received everything out of this pasture that I had for you here. It is now time to move on to the next pasture.'

This was not easy to hear at the time, but it was comforting on the inside to know that growth and development had obviously taken place. Not long after this my Pastor called me into his office and sat me down, he said, 'I believe that you need to be praying about attending Bible College, I think it is something that you need to do.' There was two intense months of praying about it and arguing with the thought of it. Why would I leave all the open doors of opportunity for me here to go and train for what I was already doing? I had more doors of opportunity to minister than most of the people that I saw graduating from Bible college. Could this be the next pasture that God had for me? Could God really want me to set off to a pasture five hundred miles away from home? After two months of arguing with the Lord, I did not win the argument. The time came that I sat Danielle down and told her that God had confirmed in my spirit that Tulsa was the pasture he was leading us to next. She had already graduated from the same school, Rhema Bible Training

Center, in 1996 and the thought of leaving everything was frustrating to her as well. She cried right there in the living room, then after praying about it the Lord also confirmed it in her heart. All that was left after that was the farewell parties, we were off to Tulsa Oklahoma.

When I arrived in Tulsa, I was committed to keeping my head down and receiving everything the Lord had brought me there to receive. If I am going to Tulsa to train for ministry, then I must be committed to be all in training for ministry. We took a trip to what they called 'Get Acquainted with Rhema Week', it was for those considering the move to see if it was the right place for them. We heard from teachers, pastors and leaders of the church and the school. I had already had a witness of the Spirit that it was the right place, but we were taking the steps to confirm the move. During one of the presentations the Bible college basketball coach came up and promoted the basketball program at the school and the success that it had enjoyed. He announced that there would be an open try out for all the possible incoming students tomorrow for all interested. Danielle looked at me and said, 'You should go, you just scored fifty points in the church league game last week.' I laughed at her and said, 'This is not church league baby, this is college ball. Plus, I did not bring any basketball shoes with me.'

Well, my beautiful wife found me some shoes and I was off to a basketball try out that I did not even want to attend. I was thirty-one years old and these were nineteen and twenty-year-old young men in the best shape of their life. There were about forty people that showed up to try out for the team. During the try out I found a zone and I made around seven three pointers in a row as well as making all the right passes and decisions with the ball. No one at the try out knew that my background was coaching high school basketball.

The coach began cutting players from forty down to thirty, then from thirty down to twenty. I was still remaining in the group of twenty, then he cut the group down to ten to have a five on five scrimmage. By now I was nearly about to get sick all over the court. I had been making other kids run for three years and watching them, not running myself. I began to see spots and get dizzy and somehow was still making shots, just not running back down the court. The assistant, Dave, who's wedding I would be in four years later, looked at me and said, 'You okay old man?' My response, 'No, not at all, get me out of here.' He laughed and then the scrimmage ended. The head coach narrowed the field to the players that he would like to see come back and play with the real team. Out of five remaining, I was left standing as one of those that made it. He came up and said, "I know you are out of shape, but I like your game. Go home and get in shape and come back when school starts to play with the guys." I said, "Coach, I am not coming here to play ball, I am coming here to get the word. I appreciate it, but I have been coaching for three years, not playing. I have no desire to get back into playing shape, but thanks for the offer."

School began, the team started practice and I had my head down in the classes to get what I thought I came for, training in the word. Then, a month later, the phone rang and it was the coach. He said, 'I would like to see you in my office after class tomorrow if you can make it.' I thought, 'man, I must have really impressed him.' I agreed to meet with him and he said, 'I know you don't have a desire to play, but I need an assistant coach, would you be interested?' Wow! This was cool! Could I be here to get all this rich teaching and still be able to do something I loved while in this pasture? Then I thought, 'maybe they will pay me to be an assistant and I could leave the Home Depot job I had just be hired for.' Then he said, 'This is strictly voluntary and for no pay, but I would like to have you.'

I had a wife and a house back in Louisiana and Rhema had a schedule that was demanding for the basketball program. I told him, 'Thanks, but no thanks, it could distract me from my purpose of coming to school.' A week later my faith filled, spirit led wife was talking to me about the offer. She said, 'You know you are supposed to be with that basketball team, don't you?' Sometimes you need someone to help push you into your next pasture. Others sometimes see things that you yourself cannot see. I walked in after class the next day and told the coach, 'You have me, and I am going to give you all of me, I am all in.'

I had gone from coaching in a small private school in Louisiana, to a boys home working with abandoned and abused boys, to now leading college men and working with the staff. I was fortunate to get to know a lot of the staff at the school and meet so many people that are still a part of my life today. I was in the head coaches wedding and in the other assistant coaches wedding and made friends from all over the world. I volunteered that first year and we traveled the country eventually losing in the national championship in Boston, and in another national championship in Ohio. We played in two separate divisions, one a secular college league and one a Bible college league. During the off season between school years, Coach called me in again to the office, and said he had been talking to the administration at the school. They offered to pay for my school second year and to pay for my housing as well. We would go on to win the National Championship the next year in Dallas Texas by the score of 86-85.

Fourteen years later, I am still enjoying

the divine connections and friendships that were a direct result from that green pasture in Tulsa, Oklahoma. I had a desire while coaching high school to win a State Championship, but there I was able to win a National Championship. God will truly give you the desires of your heart.

The time came to leave Tulsa, but I did not know where I was going and what the next pasture would be for my wife and me. Our Pastor back in Louisiana asked if we could drive down and meet with him for lunch. We agreed, and he offered me a full-time youth pastor position in our home church, as well as coordinator of all the church's outreaches. From 2003 until 2007 we were on the staff of our home church, with our head down and growing as much as we possibly could. The youth group was growing so much that we had to move into a larger room of the church. The outreaches were a huge success as well, we were reaching our region with the Gospel and it was all really exciting. I was also reinstated as president of a local outreach group that reached into over thirty public schools with the gospel.

During those four years in the green pasture of being on a full-time church staff I learned continuously and grew enormously. I was doing what I thought I could do the rest of my life. Then at the end of 2007 I began to feel frustration once again on the inside. This did not make a lot of sense to me at the time. I was getting paid a nice check every week, the youth group had three rotations in the band, we had youth services on Sunday nights and Wednesday nights. Our youth group had grown to the largest in town, why was I feeling so frustrated? As I prayed about it I knew that it was a case of being in a place that I no longer had to use my faith. The faith that accomplished all the great things, turned into just coasting and now things had appeared too easy. "You have received everything in this pasture that I had for you. It's time to go to the next green pasture." Those familiar words are the ones that I heard loud and clear. Not to leave the church, but to move on to the next pasture of growth. It was a difficult move to step down from a full time, now easy position, and remain on the front row.

When a pasture dries up for you, it may not have dried up for all the others around you. They could still be growing and developing in the same place that you have received all that was intended for you. The place is still a good place, and the land still a good land, it may just be that your time in that pasture has come to an end. Only you can know that for yourself. The Lord is your shepherd and the sons of God are led by the Spirit of God. Where he leads you, he feeds you and he grows you. When the growing stops and the pasture seems dried up for you, God has more pastures! We will all continually grow if we continue to follow his leading, and a sure indicator will be the level of feeding and development. If the pasture seems to be dried up and growth seems to be halted, begin to look for a gate and an open door, there is always more!

CHAPTER EIGHT
A COW AT A NEW GATE

Joshua 3:3-4
3 and they commanded the people, saying, "When you see the ark of the covenant of the Lord your God, and the priests, the Levites, bearing it, <u>then you shall set out from your place and go after it</u>. 4 Yet there shall be a space between you and it, about two thousand cubits by measure. Do not come near it, that you may know the way by which you must go, for <u>you have not passed this way before</u>."

Stepping into a new pasture that God has led you and into a time of transition can be hard on your flesh. Doubts can arise, as well as fear and worry about the next big move that you know you must take to follow God's plan. You are about to go places and do things that you have never done before. This is a new land of uncertainty and you have not gone this way before. Yet, your heart's desire is to follow God with your life, and you know that if he is leading you then it must be good.

In Louisiana, as I was growing up, I always heard the saying, 'Don't just sit there like a cow at a new gate, move!' The saying fits well during those times of transition. A cow has come to a new gate that it has never seen and is not quite sure what to do. Does he go in, or does he stay in the safe pasture that he knows very well and has gotten so comfortable feeding in? I'm not sure how much truth there is to how cow's respond to new gates, it may just be a saying that the old timers used to get a point across. However, I do know how I have responded at each new gate that leads to the next green pasture. I just sit for a while and stare at this next open door God has led me to, and at first I am hesitant to move out into the unknown. One thing is for certain; if you never go, then you will never know.

We all start off in life with dreams of grandeur; to see the world, go to the moon, explore the unknown like a trailblazer. Then, we get older and we are limited to our address. As a child, we began with dreams larger than life, then we fear the unknown and do not dare go where we have not gone before, calling it wisdom in our later years. I believe God will always lead you to do things that you have never done. He loves it when we are driven by a dream to accomplish the impossible.

Above we see that the children of

Israel were following the Ark of the Covenant, which represented the presence of God to them. Where the ark went is where they believed God went, and as followers of God they wanted to be where God was at. We should all have that attitude in life. Where ever God is going and where he is leading us, that is the place that we should want to be more than any other. They were encouraged to follow the presence of God, because he was going where they had never been before.

They were instructed to set out from their current position and go after the presence of God. Then they were told to keep their distance, and not move too quickly that they would know the way. When following God into the unknown there must be a time of knowing where he is going. A time of being sure and certain that you are going the right way, since you have not gone this way before. Your best place in life and your safest place in life is where God leads you.

This is walking by faith and following God's leading. We often describe faith as a blind leap out into the unknown, but it is steps we take following God's lead. Faith comes by hearing, and often this hearing is on the inside as we listen to the still small voice. A blind leap is more like taking a chance on the unknown hoping all will work out. When you have a leading and a word from God on moving into the next pasture you can know that you are going in faith. It would be foolishness to move into another pasture without knowing that God is leading you there.

The cow at a new gate is acting more

out of stubbornness than he is waiting to hear a still small voice. We can often do the same and be stubborn because we are not sure what is beyond this new open door. This stubbornness is nothing but unbelief when we refuse to move when we know that we have followed God to this new pasture.

I was once watching a friend of mine trying to get a horse into a trailer. That horse was as stubborn as he could be, and he did not want to go into that trailer. He was fighting my friend with all he had and in an all-out rebellion to obey his master. His will was as strong as he was, and if that horse did not want to go into that trailer then no one was going to force him. Then my friend had to outsmart the horse. He knew that the horse liked to eat carrots, so he tied a carrot to a string and dangled it in front of the horse just out of its reach and he led him right into the trailer. I believe God has his own unique ways of helping us when we are rebellious and stubborn when he is trying to take us places. He will never force our will, but that does not mean that he will not lead us in other ways.

For two years, I attended the church where I was saved. I helped in every area that they needed help. I was moved into leadership with vacation bible school, teaching the kids, ministering in the youth, chaperoned youth ski trips, and was given full access of the gymnasium life center there to reach out to the area youth. This church was very good to me and I had developed very strong relationships with everyone there. I loved them like they were family. Every Wednesday night they served dinner before church, and the lady over the kitchen would always save me a plate while I worked the life center. She would set it aside without fail and make sure I got extra portions. The senior adult men would have bible study in the life center on Saturday mornings and there would always be a few that would stay late and have a cup of coffee with me. There were always kids that came to the life center after school and they all waited on me to arrive with the suckers and candy that I would always stop at the store to bring them. There was nothing but love that I had for these people for the way they reached out to me and helped me in my new life in Christ.

At the end of those two years I knew that the Lord was leading me to another church in town. To this day, I believe that there are only two reasons that are legitimate reason to leave a church God puts you in to grow. One is simple, God said to leave and move on because it is in his plan. The second legitimate reason to leave a church is false doctrine being preached that could poison your spirit man. It is never okay to leave a church because someone there hurt your feelings, nor is it okay because you do not see eye to eye with the leadership. If God put you there, then these are the only two reasons that he would lead you to a new pasture and open a gate for you to go elsewhere.

God was clear when he told me my time here was over and he wanted me to move over into a new pasture where he would grow me. However, I was rebellious and stubborn refusing to leave this place that had been so good to me and the people that I had developed strong relationships with that I care about deeply. This was not something that I was willing to do, I was not going into the trailer and letting the master move me to a new place. But God had a carrot! Her name was Danielle, and she invited me to the adult Sunday school class that she would be teaching that morning, which happened to be at the church God had told me to move and start attending. She was the most beautiful person that I had ever seen teaching a bible study that is for sure. As I sat and listened to her teach on 'Touch not my Anointed', I could barely concentrate on the teaching. The only thing that I could think was, 'I am going to marry that good-looking woman! She loves God and she looks good too!' Today we have been married over eighteen years, but she began as 'God's carrot' to get this stubborn man where he was supposed to be.

God will never push us to move into the new pastures that he has for us in his plans. But he will lead us, and sometimes use any means necessary to get through our stubbornness. I thank God that he led me in those early years to get to the rich green pasture land that would be like 'miracle grow' in my spiritual journey. The teaching I received there was a word in due season and I still stand on much of that great teaching today as a faith foundation.

I have come to the place now where new gates get me excited. Going places that I have never gone before no longer scares me or worries me because I know who is leading me. I still have to fight my flesh and put it under and listen to the spirit. If God is there, then that is where I want to be. Why would I want to be in a place that

God is not leading me? He does not lead everyone to the same pasture and you must leave your place and set out to go after him. Some people and relationships you will leave, but once you step out you will only add to those divine relationships God places in your life. I am thankful for those in the first church I attended, but I am also thankful for the people God added to me in the next pasture. None more than my wife and lifetime partner! A woman full of faith and an uncompromising heart for the word of God.

It will take faith to step into these new pastures and walk through these open gates. God does not have a plan for your life that does not include faith. If you are following God, then he has already gone before you to prepare the way. There is no reason to sit there too long with a confused look on your face. You are going to have to move forward by faith, and it is going to be a good move. Don't be the one that lives life regretting what you did not do with your life. If you know, then you have to go!

When God sent the spies to spy out the land he sent them to the good land, he did not bring the good land to them. God will always bring you to your blessing, and not bring your blessing to you. He had to see if they were willing to go in and possess what he had already said belonged to them. Caleb and Joshua responded in faith, while the rest were filled with fear and doubt claiming that the people there were giants and we cannot go in. Only those that responded to the good land in faith would enter the land and experience the provision of God. The others could not see themselves there even though God had promised them the land. Their lack of faith caused them to die without receiving God's best. When God shows you something he has for you, always say, 'We are going in!' He brought you to it, how will you respond? You have not been there before, but there are things there that belong to you! If you do not go, then you will never know.

CHAPTER NINE
NEW PASTURE - NEW PROVISION

Psalm 68:19 Blessed be the Lord, who daily loads us with benefits, even the God of our salvation. Selah.

We have discussed the green pastures development and growth that takes place as we follow the Good Shepherd. However, there are many more reasons that God leads us to the pastures that he leads us into. One of the definitions of green pastures we mentioned was 'prosperous pastures'. These are pastures that cause us to advance, and as we advance with God there are benefits and provisions in front of us. The blessings that come from being in the right place at the right time.

God has plans to daily load us with his benefits and his provisions. They are not thrown out in hopes that we stumble upon them. They are strategically placed in the pastures that he has for us. My wife was not in my first pasture, she was in my third pasture. A blessing and a benefit that I would have missed if I would have decided to lay down in pasture number one. A National Championship was a benefit God had waiting for me in a pasture five hundred miles away in Tulsa. I would have missed it if I remained in Louisiana.

These daily benefits keep us filled with expectation in the green pastures. I am here so that I can get there, but I am also here to be loaded with blessings and benefits. As we are growing we keep going, and along that path are provisions God has prepared for us.

What benefit and blessing is it that God is waiting to load you up with? It is the desires of your heart and all the things that you have not yet seen, but you believe. Do not get discouraged because you have not received all that God has shown you. It only means that you have a lot of things coming. It will surely come to pass!

Genesis 2:5 Now no shrub had yet appeared on the earth and no plant had yet sprung up, for the Lord God had not sent rain on the earth and there was no man to work the ground.

Our job as we walk with God is to be in position to receive his provision. In Genesis 2:5 above we see that all was in place for man, but God did not cause increase, because man was not in position yet for the provision. God has increase waiting for us, we only need to get in position to receive. Often it is not that the blessing is not flowing, we are just in the wrong place to enjoy it. If the blessing and provision is in another pasture and we are not there, it does not mean that God is withholding from us. We must be positioned under the spout where the blessings flow out.

Now the importance of being in the green pastures that God has for us also effects the things we have in our life. Too often God gets a bad reputation for not doing what he said he would do. Nothing is farther from the truth, he is a God of his word and if he said it, then it is so. Why is it that we never honestly evaluate our own steps, to see if we are positioned properly to receive what God has promised to give? Everything man needed was always here even before the man was in position. Everything you need is already in the earth today, are you in position to receive it? If not, it is probably only a minor adjustment that is needed on your part.

Every new pasture has all new provision. We moved our family to Florida in 2010 to pioneer a church. I told the Lord one day, 'I don't know anyone in Florida.' He said, 'That's okay, I know everyone in Florida.' Our job was to leave Louisiana and reposition ourselves to Florida. We are so blessed and thankful that we followed him to our green Florida pasture. He had everything here waiting on us to arrive. There was a church here on the verge of closing the doors and God told us we were to pastor that church and not start our own. There was only a hand full of people and at first, we were not real excited about it. We have since experienced a daily loading of God's benefits and blessings. Not only the people that have crossed our path have been a blessing, but everything was in place before we arrived.

In 2010 the church was meeting in a hotel room on Sunday mornings, and in a member's house on Wednesday nights. When we transitioned into the role of Pastor, we learned that they had a storage building filled with equipment, chairs, children's ministry materials and more. It was enough for us to find a standalone building of our own and start with what was already here. After six years of being in this Florida pasture, God has proven faithful to provide! We recently purchased a two-million-dollar facility that we bought for only one million dollars. It is a thirty thousand square foot building with plenty of room to grow. It was empty and for sale nearly two years while we were in our first building preparing to position for the provision. It was sitting there all along waiting for us to get into position.

You could say that it's all a set up. God is setting you up for everything he has prepared for you. Psalm 23 says that *he prepares a table before us*, meaning the provision and benefits are on the table, the only thing missing is you. Take your place and enjoy the preparations, they are all for you. God has been expecting you!

CHAPTER TEN
PERFECT PASTURE

Perfect God

Hebrews 6:13 For when God made a promise to Abraham, because He could swear by no one greater, He swore by Himself, 14 saying, "Surely blessing I will bless you, and multiplying I will multiply you."

Malachi 3:6 For I am the Lord, I do not change.

There is nothing like knowing that you are in your perfect pasture and where you are is perfect. To many, they believe this is not possible. Believing that they could never reach a perfect place. The good news is that you can find your perfect place and it is in God's perfect will. The urgency in writing this book is that if you are not in your perfect place and in God's perfect will, you will find that perfect place quickly.

This world that we live in is changing all the time. It was only a little over a hundred years ago, that the pony express was delivering messages across the country on horseback. Now, we can video chat with people on the other side of the world in real time. We have gone from rotary phones and phone booths, to smart phones that can do nearly everything that we need.

In this changing world, there are constants that never change. One of those constants that never change is our God. When he made the promise to Abraham he could swear by no greater, so he swore by himself. In Malachi, he tells us that he is the Lord and he does not change. Why doesn't

God change? He is perfect and he cannot be improved or upgraded.

There is nothing that our God does not know. He is all knowing and has never had a new idea. There is never anything that can arise that he did not already know. He is perfection is every way, and he is living inside of every believer. He knows the future better than we know the past.

He does not change, not because he is stubborn and hard headed, but because you cannot improve on perfection. He is a perfect God, a perfect Father and a perfect leader. He is leading us to our perfect place, a perfect pasture that exists for every one of us.

We often want God to change and become like us, because we do not want to change. He is not going to change, so we must change to become more like him. Yes, on the inside, the perfect one lives inside of us, but the perfect one wants to work his perfection out of us. There is something on the inside working on the outside. His perfect love is shed abroad in our hearts, but it must show up in our daily lives. His perfect joy is in our hearts, but it must show up on our face.

How many people simply refuse to change? They have always been this way and refuse to make any adjustments. They have always done it this way, so they see no reason to change it now. These same people are often frustrated with how things are going in their life. We would all do well to let the God of perfection complete the good work he has begun in us. The

Bible tells us 'Be ye perfect, for I am perfect', it also tells us 'to aim for perfection'. One of the definitions of perfect is to be completely matured. To mature we must grow continually. In our green pastures where God has placed us, there is a place of perfecting and maturing. When God perfects you and grows you there, then he moves on to perfecting you in other areas. The more we fellowship with and follow the perfect God, he perfects us and matures us. We aim for the place that we are complete and entire lacking nothing.

Psalms 138:8 The Lord will perfect that which concerns me;

God's work is to complete us and to perfect us. In every stage and in every pasture the God that cannot be upgraded is upgrading us and perfecting all things that concern us. Your perfect place is your perfecting place. You are the offspring of perfection! Perfection is your daddy! You have been born of incorruptible seed. Your father is the great I AM. He has deposited his perfect Spirit on the inside of you and has a perfect plan for your life.

Perfect Word

Psalms 19:7 The law of the Lord is perfect, reviving the soul;

Psalms 18:30 As for God, His way is perfect; The word of the Lord is proven;

Deuteronomy 12:32 Whatever my word commands you, you shall be careful to do; you shall not add to nor take away from it.

Just like God cannot be upgraded or improved, his word is perfection. God chose to send his perfect word to perfect our lives. We all need the revelation that every time we pick up a Bible we are picking up perfection. It cannot be added to or taken away from or it then becomes imperfect. In Isaiah 55 God says that his ways are higher than our ways and his thoughts are higher than our thoughts. Like the rain comes down, so does my word, it will not return void. His perfect word and his perfect ways have come down.

I have heard countless people say that they do not believe certain parts of God's word, yet it does not make it any less perfect. Picking and choosing which parts we want to believe from God's word is a foolish thing to do. It is complete and entire, so neglecting areas of God's word will leave us incomplete. I have known many believers that love 1 Corinthians chapter 13, which is known as the love chapter. They also love 1 Corinthians chapter 15, which speaks about the return of the Lord and the catching away of the church. These same people avoid 1 Corinthians 14, and they claim that this chapter is not for today. They say that tongues and the infilling of the Holy Spirit was only for the early apostles and it is not needed today. These believers will never be complete and entire lacking nothing. They take away from God's word and do not take it at face value. I like to say that there are some people who are highlighter believers, and other believers who are white-out believers. No, if it is in the word of God, it is there to perfect you and to mature you.

I was sitting on the couch the other day and my phone vibrated to alert me that my bible app was in the process of updating. I laughed and I thought, 'Is there another chapter now?' I knew it was probably updating the features of the app, but God's word never requires an update. In the United States, we have made many amendments to our constitution, but throughout all of eternity God's word will never require any amendments. It is perfection.

The Lord as our shepherd leads us with his word, his perfect word. The sheep follow the voice of the shepherd, and the voice of a stranger they will not follow. His word is not given only for doctrine, but also for perfecting. Leading us into our perfect place.

Ephesians 4:11-12
11 And he gave some, apostles; and some, prophets; and some, evangelists; and some, pastors and teachers; 12 For the <u>perfecting</u> of the saints, for the work of the ministry, for

the edifying of the body of Christ:

God's intent for all the fivefold ministry gifts is for the perfecting of the saints, to do the work of the ministry, for the edifying of the body of Christ. These are voices that speak into our lives the perfect word of God, thus perfecting and maturing our lives. I like to think of these fivefold ministry gifts as echoes that repeat what they hear from the great shepherd. Jesus said, 'I only say what I hear the Father say.' He was an echo of the perfect father, to relay to us his perfect word.

Some say that they would follow Jesus, but no man would they ever follow. These people will never be perfected and fully mature. God chose these gifts as his assistants to equip and perfect his followers. They claim that they receive enough word at home on the couch, and do not need to be a part of any organized church, or under any church leaders. The truth is that there are some things God will never tell you at home, some things he will only give you through the gifts that he gave to his body. It is not the only way we are perfected, but it is one of the ways God chose to perfect us. Humbling ourselves under God's mighty hand, on that hand is five fingers. It is a sign of humility to receive God's perfect word he has placed in an imperfect vessel.

This perfect God delivers to us his perfect word that transforms our lives that brings us to his perfect will and his perfect place!

Perfect Will / Perfect Pasture

*Romans 12:2 And be not conformed to this world: but be ye transformed by the renewing of your mind, that ye may prove what is that good, and acceptable, and **<u>perfect will</u>** of God.*

If there is not a perfect will and a perfect place, then the word of God would not tell us such a place exist. This scripture says that we can conform to the world, or we can transform into God's perfect will. This is our perfect pasture and it is in God's perfect will. We find this place in our life as we transform our mind to his perfect word. It is perfect plan by a perfect God.

The transforming of the mind results in a transformation of our actions. As our actions transform we then develop and mature, being perfected in each pasture of life. I believe just knowing that there is a perfect place for us all is a call for rejoicing. Why settle for good when perfect is available.

God's green pastures are all your perfect places in life. Your happy place! My heart's desire is that you will find your perfect place, by finding his perfect will, which is found in his perfect word. The transformation will be a process, but it will be a good process. The moment that the transformation begins to take place is the moment that you are in his process of perfection.

There is nothing better than knowing you are in God's perfect place for your life. He is perfecting that which concerns you in your current perfect pasture and he is leading you to your next place of perfecting. Once the transformation in this pasture is complete there is only more perfect places in your future.

You are where you are, so that God can get you to where you are going. If God led you here, then he is taking you to there. Here and now you are in God's perfect place of his perfect process of transformation. No longer conform, but allow God to transform you in each pasture. If you are there, then be all there. Since you are in, then be all in. This transformation can be slow or it can be rapid. This is determined by you and only by you. Throw off any old ways and thoughts formed by the world. Any old habits and work ethics and attitudes adapted by the world around you. These only prevent us from living in our perfect place.

If you are not in God's perfect green pasture for your life, then make the necessary adjustments. Don't spend another minute in a place that is not the perfect place for you. All of God's perfect blessings that he has pre-ordained for your life are sitting in your perfect pasture. Your very best days have not yet happened. You are going from glory to glory and changing at every stage, in every pasture.

In closing, know that God loves you dearly and has specific plans for your life. He knows the very number of hairs on your head and wrote all your days in a book before one came to be. His plan is that you have life and have it in abundance. I believe you will find that plan of abundance and you will hear the voice of our good shepherd and the voice of a stranger you will not follow. You will experience no lack on your journey. You will always be in the right place, at the right time, with all the right people.

The Lord is your shepherd you shall not lack. You will enjoy all of his 'Green Pastures'.

Making God your Father

You may have read this book and you do not know God as your Father. Becoming a child of God is simple, all that is required is faith to ask. Pray this prayer now and receive your place in the Father's family:

"Father God, I come to you by faith right now. Your word says that if I believe in my heart, and I confess with my mouth, that Jesus is Lord, I will be saved. I do believe, and I do confess, that Jesus is now Lord of my life. I am now a child of God, and God is now forever my Father. Thank you for loving me and accepting me into your family."

ABOUT THE AUTHOR

Roddy Shaffer is from Minden Louisiana and currently the Senior Pastor of Living Faith Christian Center in Niceville, Florida. He was born again September 19, 1995 after a radical encounter with a loving God. He immediately began preaching God's word, using his coaching platform to minister to his local area, then the Lord called him to full time ministry in 1998. He was married to his wife Danielle in November of 1998 and has two children Julia and Jake. He has passion for the Word of God and seeing the lost saved and the prodigal wayward children restored back to abundant life with the Father. He also has a passion to see the Body of Christ equipped to rise and be all that God has called them to be In Christ. He is a 2003 graduate of Rhema Bible Training Center in Tulsa Oklahoma. He ministers nationally and internationally proclaiming the Good News.

Made in the USA
Columbia, SC
04 June 2021